NITON PUBLISHING

MERCEDES-BENZ

IN PICTURES

ROY BACON

First published in 1999 by Niton Publishing
P.O. Box 3, Ventnor, Isle of Wight, PO38 2AS

Acknowledgements
All photographs in this publication were supplied by the National Motor Museum, Beaulieu. Our thanks go to all the photographers who stood behind their cameras to record the history shown here.

A CIP catalogue record for this book is available from the British Library.

ISBN 1 85579 039 4

Design by : Roy Bacon and Joseph Murphy
Printed through World Print, Hong Kong

Title page: The fully-streamlined W196 of 1954 that marked the return of Mercedes-Benz to grand prix racing. More usually run in open form, it won first time out and took Fangio to two world titles.

Front cover: Fabulous 1955 300SL Gullwing Coupe.
Rear cover: Prewar advertisement from the 1930s.

MERCEDES-BENZ
THREE-POINTED STAR

When Mercedes linked with Benz in 1926 both firms already had good reputations and had more than made their marks. Karl Benz built his first machine in 1886 at Mannheim and went on to produce a series of models during the late-Victorian era. Soon after the start of the new century they had the engine at the front driving the rear wheels in what became the conventional form for many decades, and went on to built a good range of cars in various forms. Among them was a powerful road model that became used for speed work, while postwar there came a mid-engined racing car that foretold the future in its layout, but only appeared once.

The origins of Mercedes lay with Gottlieb Daimler who built a motorcycle in 1885 as an engine test bed and then went on to four wheels and through the same transition from horse-drawn carriage to motor car as Benz. By 1901 their car had the then norm of engine at the front behind a radiator, four-speed gearbox, steel chassis and rear-wheel drive. It was called Mercédès after the daughter of a Daimler agent, and its lines were truly those of a motor car. In a year the Daimler name had gone, exported to Britain where it remains in use, and Mercedes were already making a name in the long distance, town to town races of the time. Other successes followed, culminating in their win in the 1914 French Grand Prix and in the Indianapolis 500 in 1915.

Postwar, Ferdinand Porsche was chief designer for Mercedes and developed their supercharged engines. These helped the firm back into competition in events such as the Targa Florio but both they and Benz found trading conditions tough. So they amalgamated as Daimler-Benz of Stuttgart with the cars sold as the Mercedes-Benz just as now.

At first they built prosaic saloons but these were soon joined by some classic sports cars, supercharged and with wonderful lines. The firm went motor racing again to win the German GP three years in succession, but it was from 1934 that they, and Auto Union, dominated the grand prix scene with their fantastic cars.

The firm struggled back onto its feet in 1946 with an improved prewar saloon that was simple, basic and just what was needed. Others followed and by 1950 the range included a luxury model for that expanding market. They returned again to competition to run and win at Le Mans in 1952 and this led to the 300SL 'Gullwing' production car two years later. By then they had joined the grand prix scene, first with fully streamlined cars that won first time out, and then with more conventional models that took them to two world titles. They were equally successful in the 1955 Mille Miglia but at the end of the season they left the scene.

By the end of the decade the saloon and coupé models had become dated so a new style was introduced. As would become common practice, the one style was offered with a range of engine sizes and was soon joined by a sporting coupé that had similar options but wore its own style. While it became Mercedes-Benz practice to list longer versions of their saloons, these were quite overshadowed by the massive 600 which was big, or bigger with six doors. It stood alone from the range while this expanded and developed on its established lines, seldom radical as to looks, but always leading in technical and safety areas.

So it was into the 1990s when the blower returned for the Kompressor model that carried its three-pointed star as well and as proudly as any of the glorious Silver Arrows.

Gottlieb Daimler assisted Dr. Otto before moving to Cannstatt with Wilhelm Maybach where they built a motorcycle in 1885 as a trial machine for an engine. In the next year they installed a 462cc single-cylinder in the vehicle shown here that used the chassis from an American carriage supplied by Wimpff & Sohn of Stuttgart. The engine was mounted vertically behind the front seat so here sits between Daimler's feet as he takes his ease.

By 1889 Daimler and Maybach had moved on to this Stahlrad-Wagen propelled by a 565cc V-twin engine that drove the back axle by gear wheels with a choice of four ratios. There was a differential in the axle next to the right-hand wheel and a band brake for the left. The chassis was built by the firm that later became NSU and its steel tubes carried the cooling water. The wheels were constructed in steel, from which the name came, and the front ones held in linked bicycle forks.

Karl Benz built his first three-wheeler in 1886 as a complete vehicle, the frame made by Adler cycles. His 984cc engine had a single horizontal cylinder and vertical crankshaft, with bevel gears, flat-belt pulleys, a countershaft and a chain on each side to drive the rear wheels. Strictly functional, it went on a 180 km trip two years later, driven by Berta Benz, Karl's wife, accompanied by two of their sons.

Benz lived in Mannheim where his early work led to this Benz-Wagen of 1891. The engine remained under the rear seat with chain drive to the wheels, the chassis showed its horse-carriage origins and the Vis-à-Vis body, where the occupants faced each other, was sociable but impaired driver vision.

By 1890 Daimler had produced this machine. Its engine remained at the rear with gear drive to the wheels, the front axle was pivoted at the centre as for a wagon, while this example had a Vis-à-Vis body.

The Cannstatt-Daimler cars were so named from their factory location on the outskirts of Stuttgart with this 1892 model using the V-twin engine and having chain drive to the rear wheels, the fronts still with their linked bicycle forks and no suspension. Block brakes on the rears arrested the vehicle from its 20 km/h top speed.

The Benz Victoria was built from 1893 to 1900 and powered by a 1725cc single-cylinder engine that grew to 2915cc by 1898. Gears, flat-belts and chains were included in the two-speed transmission and the model introduced stub-axle steering with front and rear wheels sprung by double-elliptical springs. The suspension attached directly to the body, in this case a Vis-à-Vis type of 1894 with Karl and Berta Benz plus friends aboard.

The lighter Benz Velo appeared in 1893 fitted with a 1142cc single-cylinder engine and the two-speed transmission of the Victoria, but later versions, built up to 1902, had three speeds and reverse using planetary gears. This early example carried two and had Clara Benz at the wheel, but other forms were also built.

The Benz family en mass in 1895 with a Velo ahead of a Victoria. In front were daughters Clara and Thilde, behind came son Richard, in the uniform of his military service, and relatives of the Benz family on a visit to Mannheim.

The horse-carriage ancestry is most noticeable with this Benz Motor Wagen of 1894 where the driver sits up front, just as the coachman did, with the passengers facing each other in the main body. The engine remained at the rear with chain drive to the wheels.

In 1895 the Cannstatt-Daimler still had the V-twin engine, centre pivot front axle and Vis-à-Vis body form. Few cars were built in the early-1890s and commercial problems inhibited progress despite other firms having used Daimler engines in the past.

Taken at the Crystal Palace in 1895, a Benz Victoria-Familie model with Vis-à-Vis seating, rear engine and chain drive. Mr Hewetson was the driver at a time when most cars in England were demonstrated in private grounds or subject to harassment on open roads. His passenger, Mrs Bazalgette, was the only lady driver to take part in the 1,000-mile trial held in 1900 when she drove a Benz Ideal.

A Daimler Landau of the 1890s with separate hoods for each pair of Vis-à-Vis seats. The driver sat out front above the engine that drove back to a gearbox from which a shaft ran to a rear cross-shaft. A small pinion at each end of this drove an internal gear attached to each rear wheel.

A Benz Velo from the late-1890s used by Hewetson's, the sole British agents for the make, and fitted with a small van body that enabled it to act as a service vehicle and advertise the marque. A useful combination of jobs that could fit in well with the horse-drawn traffic of late-Victorian London.

Another body form for the Benz Victoria was this omnibus built from around 1895. Able to carry eight passengers, it had a 5hp engine of 2650cc, but still only one cylinder, to cope with both them and their luggage.

The first Cannstatt-Daimler imported into England in 1895 with Frederick Simms at the wheel. Earlier, Simms imported Daimler engines and later worked with Robert Bosch on magnetos, built his own engine for others, and produced an odd tricycle in 1900. This had two driven wheels at the front and one for steering at the back and was not a success, but his engines and electrical products were produced for years and he was a major figure in transport.

Cycles, motorcycles, machinery and cars were all the same to Glover Bros. in late-Victorian times when a good engineer could turn his hand to anything. Here they have new cycles to unpack from a crate, a Benz needing fuel or attention, and a Panhard ready to move off.

The Paul Daimler car of 1899, also known as the PD-Wagen, that was built in the firm's Austrian subsidiary pointed the way to the future with the engine at the front while retaining the chain drive to the rear wheels.

The older Cannstatt-Daimler in its 1895 form with Vis-à-Vis seating, a roof for the occupants, curtains at the back and a fringe for the top. Reflecting the horse-and-buggy era in a delightful way with its centre-pivot front axle, but already dated.

It was 1904 when number plates were first required on motor vehicles registered in Britain and CR was allocated to Southampton where it stayed. The car is a Benz Velo and carries the nameplate of a dealer of that town, so by then it was some years old. The tricycle is older and enjoys the fitment of a full chaincase.

In place of the hansom cab and other conveyances for hire there came this Daimler Taxameter of 1898 to carry you through the park. Licensed to carry four, facing each other, it had a weight limit and a cab number stencilled on the side. The lady's hat would limit the speed.

The 1899 Benz Dos-à-Dos model had a 1728cc flat-twin engine, and three forward speeds plus reverse using a belt and chain transmission. Later models had a larger engine while the model name referred to the back-to-back seating for the four occupants. This was none too sociable, although it did give the driver a better view of the road, but was soon replaced by having all the seats facing forward.

The Daimler Phoenix of 1899 introduced the more modern concept of four cylinders for its 5507cc engine, a radiator cooling system, clutch, four speeds, differential, chassis frame and suspension springs set along the frame. Only in the use of chains to drive the rear wheels and the dos-à-dos seating did the past really survive.

E.J. Coles was a brave man to attempt this 'Fancy Driving' with his Benz Velo in 1900 with its meagre block brakes. Could be that the left rear wheel was chained down for the camera exposure. The location was the Agricultural Hall in London while the Hewetson service van stands at the rear, either to reassure possible Benz buyers or to help Coles if need be.

A Benz at the turn of the century when the firm of Benz & Cie. Rheinische Gasmotorenfabrik AG was the largest car factory in the world. However, sales fell dramatically in 1901 for car design had moved on and the old Benz, with its horse-carriage ancestry, was outmoded.

In 1900 a 1,000-Mile Trial was held from London to Scotland and back to demonstrate that the car was a practical alternative to the horse. It was run by the Automobile Club, later the RAC, in ten daily stages and the sole lady driver was Mrs Bazalgette who had a trial run in a Benz at Crystal Palace in 1895. In the lengthy event she drove a Benz Ideal and completed the course.

This Benz of 1900 had the flat-twin engine driving a four-speed and reverse gearbox but kept the chain final drive and horse-carriage style. The neat coupé body did give shelter to its occupants but the driver remained out in the weather in coach style.

Gottlieb Daimler died in March 1900, wearied by problems at the firm, but Wilhelm Maybach then created a new model for Emil Jellinek. It had to be light and fast as well as stylish and the result was named after his daughter, Mercedes; and thus a legend was born. This is a 1901 racing model that proved itself in the Nice-Salon-Nice race that year, after problems at Pau a month earlier, and went on to be the fastest petrol car over the flying kilometer and winner of La Turbie hill climb over the next few days, Christian Werner the driver.

In one move the Daimler firm went from the horse carriage to a modern format when they introduced the Mercedes in 1901. The following year brought this Simplex version that continued with the layout of front-mounted 6786cc four-cylinder engine cooled by the Maybach honeycomb radiator, four-speed gearbox with gate change and light, steel frame. Except for the chain final drive it was the format for the future.

Taken in 1932, this is a 1900 Benz in the Haymarket, London, advertising Harold Lloyd movies being shown at the Carlton Theatre. A double played the part of Lloyd while the driver enjoyed the warmth and comfort of his coat.

The same Benz, credited as 1901, on Westminster Bridge during an early Brighton run with a Green Line bus passing it en-route to Reigate. The car has its offside wheels stuck in the tramline, always a hazard with narrow section tyres.

Taken at the start of the last of the big inter-town races, the tragic Paris-Madrid event of 1903 that was terminated at Bordeaux after many accidents. Here, Degrais waits to go in his 90hp Mercedes that would finish 39th of the Heavy cars and 69th in the general classification after just over 10-hours driving.

Taken during the 1903 Paris-Madrid race, this is Gasteaux in a 60hp Mercedes that would finish 7th in the Heavy car class after six hours at the wheel. The stones beside the road were there to fill potholes in the surface while spectators on this climb remained close to the action.

This 1901 Benz showed where the car had come from for, despite the front bonnet, the engine remained at the rear, the transmission a combination of belts and chains, the wheels with wooden spokes and the body in a carriage style.

One of the 90hp Mercedes cars in the 1903 Paris-Madrid race was driven by Jenatzy, known as 'The Red Devil' on account of his red beard and meteoric driving style. Here, he and his mechanic carry out engine repairs after which they continued to finish 11th in the Heavy car class.

Baron De Caters at the Virage de Petignac during the 1903 Paris-Madrid race in which he drove one of the 90hp Mercedes cars to 20th place in the Heavy car class. More stone piles at the roadside for repair work.

After Paris-Madrid in 1903 races were held on closed, but lengthy, circuits with the Gordon-Bennett event of that year being run in Ireland. Mercedes had to use their 60hp cars as all but one of the 90hp models had perished in a major fire at the Cannstatt works in June 1903 which meant a move to Untertürkheim in 1904. In Ireland Camille Jenatzy won for Mercedes by ten minutes from De Knyff after six hours of hard driving.

A modified 1902 40hp Mercedes owned by Baron Henri de Rothschild and fitted with a special body to reduce wind resistance. Under it went an engine with two twin-cylinder blocks with their heads in aluminium while final drive remained by chain and would continue as such on the 60 and 90hp cars of 1903.

The 1902 Benz brought the firm up to date in that its 2945cc engine went at the front along with the radiator to drive back to the gearbox and thence to the rear wheels. But, it remained a flat-twin when Daimler had an in-line four, and kept the chain final drive then usual. This example was fitted with an eight-seater body but two or four-seat styles were more common.

By 1904 the Mercedes Simplex had lost the horse-carriage image and had the real style of the automobile. In the fashion of the decade it remained a luxury form of travel with seats to suit but performance had increased to require the hood stays while the famous three-pointed star had appeared on the radiator.

In May 1904 Baron de Caters set the kilometer record to 97.25 mph using this 90hp Mercedes, taking it but soon losing it for five men broke the record that year. The Mercedes won it and then lost it to Rigolly whose Gobron-Brillié became the first to exceed 100 mph. The Baron stands fourth from the left with Jenatzy second from left.

This 60hp Mercedes Diligence of 1903 was first owned by Emil Jellinek whose daughter's name graced the cars and then the marque from 1901 to today. He had been a merchant in North Africa but later became an Austrian Consul-General in Nice and a society figure in that town.

This 40hp Benz of 1905 had the touring body and was also known as the Prinz Heinrich-Wagen. With it had come a move forward to four cylinders and shaft drive back to a countershaft although chains still took the power to the rear wheels.

Said to be the Royal Mercedes in which Kaiser Wilhelm rode and from around 1905. The extensive hood offered both privacy and good protection from the elements while the fittings such as headlights and horn remained as ornate as ever.

The 18/22hp Mercedes of around 1904 fitted with a full windscreen and furled hood. No wipers then or for some time to come so the screen could be removed if required while breakage would be a danger. Right-hand operation for the gate-change gearbox, floor pedals and a steering wheel carrying the horn bulb.

Prinz Ludwig Ferdinand von Bayern with a guide out in a Benz in 1905. Under the frame a sprag was still fitted to hold the car on steep hills in case the brakes should not be able to cope. The hood had a rigid top so its sides would form a closed frame to offer full enclosure.

Circuit d'Auvergne. Coupe Gordon Bennett 1905

L'Hirondelle, Paris WERNER (Mercédès) Allemagne

In 1905 the Gordon-Bennett race was held during July on the Auvergne circuit in France and six Mercedes were entered, three each for the German and Austrian teams. These 120hp cars were driven by De Caters, Braun, Jenatzy, Burton, Hieronymus and Werner, seen here, who was the best-placed German at fifth, an hour behind the winner.

The Mercedes-Rennwagen of 1905 developed from the 90hp model that had won the 1903 Gordon-Bennett race and finished a close second in 1904 with Jenatzy the driver in each event. The firm had the problem of the 1903 fire and factory move to contend with but moved on from this car to the 120hp type.

For the 1905 Gordon-Bennett race Mercedes ran the 120hp cars developed from the older type with a larger engine, longer wheelbase, more compact four-speed gearbox, but still with chain final drive and no suspension spring damping. Austria and Germany both ran teams of three cars but fifth was the best they could do. At the wheel is Otto Salzer who drove for the firm from 1906 to 1914.

The Mercedes limousine used by King Edward VII in 1905 and similar to that of the Kaiser. The high rear seat would make him more visible to his people and the enclosure kept him out of the British weather his chauffeur would have to endure. The King was an early motoring enthusiast who had bought a British Daimler as early as 1900.

An American special of 1905 based on a Mercedes 60hp model stretched to accommodate a second engine and called 'Flying Dutchman II' by driver Herbert Bowden who drove it at Daytona to 105.3 mph and then 109.8 mph, the first taken as a world's record, the second not recognised but certainly quick. Daytona Beach remained a popular venue for such attempts up to 1935 and around 300 mph.

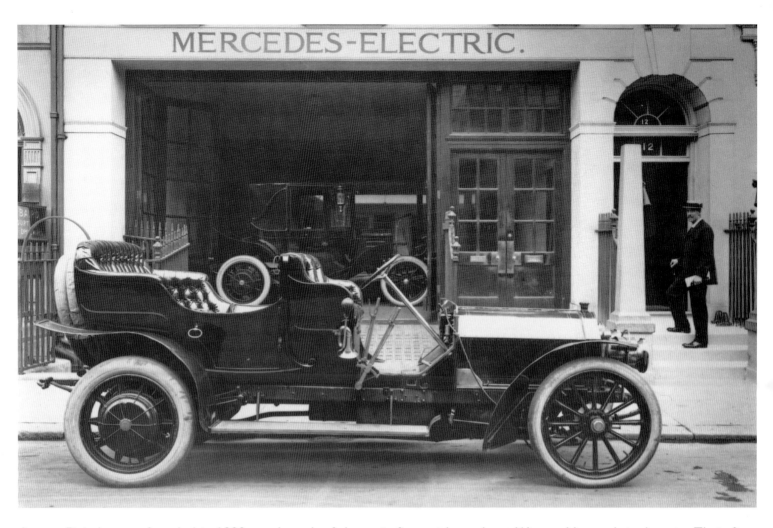

Austro-Daimler was founded in 1899 as a branch of the main firm with works at Wiener-Neustadt in Austria. Their first designer was Paul Daimler but by 1906, when they became independent, Ferdinand Porsche had replaced him. Porsche introduced this Mercedes-Mixte that employed his proven design combining a petrol engine with an electric generator that powered electric motors in the rear wheels.

A magnificent Mercedes fitted with a long body able to carry three rows of people so six or seven could travel together. Various engines were offered, the 18/28 and 40/45hp the most popular with both giving ample performance on the roads of the time.

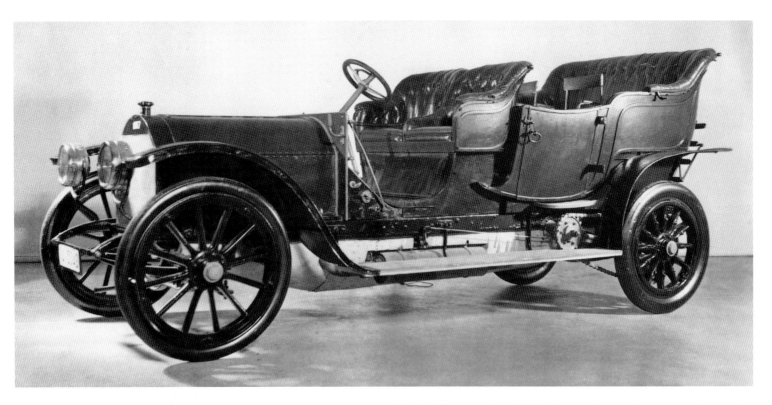

The 45/50hp open tourer of 1907 continued on the lines established by the first 1901 Mercedes with its long, low style that brought the centre of gravity down, plus its careful design to reduce weight without sacrificing strength. It was this combination that made them so successful.

By 1906 Mercedes had introduced a six-cylinder engine for their production cars by adding a third two-cylinder block to a longer crankcase. In 1905 they had an experimental car powered by a 13-litre, 135hp six engine, but this model was rated at a more modest 120hp.

One of the 1908 Grand Prix Mercedes cars seen in the public enclosure by the Finishing Straight at Brooklands. Behind is the Test Hill rising up the Members Hill with the banking in the background, the car with a 1909 registration number and the scene pre-Great War.

A Benz Phaeton with its rear hood down to bring fresh air into the passenger compartment. The driver now had a windscreen with a panel ahead that could be opened to improve visibility in poor conditions. The four-cylinder engine was rated as 14/18hp, the artillery wheels remained, but the rear drive chains had been replaced by a shaft.

This Mercedes belonged to Kaiser Wilhelm II, cousin to George V of Britain and Czar Nicholas of Russia, so carried the royal crest on the rear door and had a second windscreen as well as the large hood to enclose the passenger quarters.

Left: The major race of 1908 was the French Grand Prix and both Benz and Mercedes entered a team of three cars. This is Fritz Erle waiting for the start by his Benz that he was to bring home seventh, astern of his team-mates who were second and third.

Taken during the 1908 French Grand Prix, this picture shows Lautenschlager changing a tyre at the pits. These really were a trench dug in front of the main stand and saw much work during the race for the road surface and high speeds had many drivers changing all four tyres on each 47.74-mile lap. Tyres ran short but Lautenschlager drove steadily to preserve his and came home the winner by nine minutes.

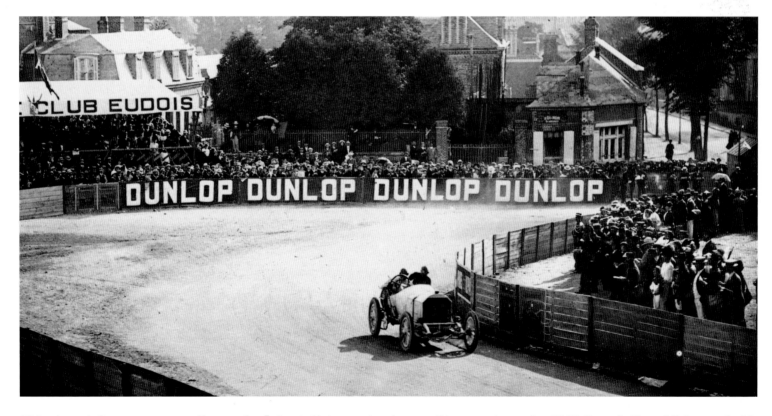

This sharp left corner was at Eu, on the Seine Inférieure circuit near Dieppe where the 1908 French Grand Prix was held, and the scene of many incidents, one involving Hémery who finished second on his Benz. Here, Salzer takes his Mercedes close in to the apex of the corner but was destined to retire after his second lap, having set the fastest for the race at 78.44 mph on his first.

Victor Hémery working on his Benz at the pits during the 1908 French Grand Prix in which he finished second after many tyre changes and an incident at the sharp corner in Eu where he arrived too fast, skidded, stalled and was nearly rammed by Pièrron driving a Motobloc who later retired after three laps.

The 1908 Benz Grand Prix car that ran in the Grand Prize of the Automobile Club of America race held at Savannah in Georgia in November 1908 where a 16-lap race was run over a 25.13-mile circuit. Victor Hémery finished second, under one minute behind the winner after over six hours racing, and another Benz was fourth.

Fine picture of Lautenschlager and his Mercedes leaving the Eu corner during the 1908 French Grand Prix which he won. The race was very hard on tyres and the Mercedes pit ran out of them two laps from the end but steady driving and a slower final lap kept Lautenschlager out of trouble.

In 1909 the Blitzen-Benz was built for speed events with a massive 21.5-litre four-cylinder engine having overhead valves and twin sparking plugs for each cylinder. It developed some 200 bhp at 1,500 rpm and drove a four-speed gearbox with chain final drive. Stub exhausts suited its purpose.

The Blitzen-Benz was taken to Brooklands in November, 1909, where Victor Hémery set World records for the standing-start half-mile, kilometer and mile at speeds ranging from 70 mph to over 87 mph for the longest distance. He then lapped the circuit in a clockwise direction when he set the World mile figure to 115.9 mph and covered the half-mile at just under 128 mph, the difference caused by the need to slow for the bankings.

A Benz 200 was built in 1913 for the British agent, L.G. Hornstead, based on the original Blitzen-Benz. Late that year he drove it at Brooklands to set World standing-start records for the half-mile and the kilometer on December 22nd. Two months before the Great War began he used the same car to set the World fastest speed to 124.1 mph where it would stay for some time. Behind the car is the Test Hill, another facet of the track.

The Blitzen-Benz was taken to the USA for 1910 and carried the imperial eagle in black on its white body. Barney Oldfield drove it at Daytona Beach, where he claimed a record speed of over 131 mph, and at many circuits where it impressed all who saw it. In 1911 it ran at Daytona again, driven by Bob Burman and a speed of 141 mph was claimed.

By 1908 Mercedes were offering shaft drive as an alternative to the chains and two years later added the windscreen. This is a 40/45hp coupé model from that period with the bonnet removed to show the four-cylinder engine.

Right: A highly ornate Mercedes limousine from pre-Great War days with a wonderful line to its entire body. Owned by one Mr Majzub, it indicates both a wish to be noticed and a wallet deep enough to indulge this taste. Underneath went the best of the firm's technical work.

One of the 1910 Mercedes models was the 38/70hp four-cylinder. In this example the chain final drive was retained but encased to keep the chains out of view with the cases able to move with the suspension. The four-seater touring body was by Moss Brothers of Fulham, London, and included a viewing panel in the side of the bonnet.

The last of the big, chain-driven Mercedes cars was the 'Ninety', introduced in 1910 with three overhead valves, one inlet and two exhaust, for each of its four cylinders. The radiator was V-shaped so carried two of the three-pointed stars, and this example from 1912 had a Prince Henry, four-seater touring body.

Up to 1912 only the major French race was called a Grand Prix but that year saw a Belgium Grand Prix, although it was actually a reliability trial. Here, a Mercedes leads another car over a bridge during the event, watched by a good crowd of spectators, the start area in the background.

A Benz Phaeton with a fully-enclosed compartment for the passengers but less protection for the driver. Built for 1911 to 1913 and powered by a 25/65hp four-cylinder engine with four speeds and shaft final drive. Still with artillery wheels and rear-wheel brakes only.

The Prince Henry Trials were held for several years up to 1911 by when they had become a tour of stately homes in Britain and Germany. This Benz was taking part in the last with a full complement of four men and a dog.

A Mercedes taking part in the 1912 Belgium Grand Prix that was run as a reliability trial. Typical pavé surface for the road alongside the river with the railway bridge over both and the results board facing the crowd.

The 28/95 Mercedes was built in small numbers before the Great War and in larger ones up to 1924 powered by a six-cylinder, overhead-camshaft engine. The engine design was based on one produced for aero use and it was also related to the race engine of 1914. This early example had chain final drive but shaft drive was soon common and various body styles were built.

At the start of the 1912 Belgium Grand Prix that was run as a reliability trial so time for this Mercedes driver and passenger to chat to the officials. Unlike a race, there would be little of the pre-event tension usual at the start when drivers would try to take their minds off the impending fall of the flag.

A 12hp Benz from around 1912 by when the design had settled down and the chain drive to the rear wheels had gone. No front brakes were deemed necessary at that time and the side-light wiring seems to be an after-thought.

Taken in 1914, this photograph shows Charles and Margot Weir on their honeymoon and parked outside the home of Charle's uncle, Henry Murray, in Ardnaveigh, near Antrim in Northern Ireland. The car is a Mercedes from that period.

The Mercedes 28/95hp model built prewar and after to 1924. It had a 7273cc six-cylinder, overhead-camshaft engine producing 90 bhp at 1,800 rpm and a four-speed gearbox. A modified car of this type finished second in the 1921 Targa Florio driven by Max Sailer who also drove all the way to Sicily in his race car. Four-wheel brakes had arrived and were a real aid in the race.

This 1912 Benz had a coupé body by the Grosvenor Carriage firm of Euston Road, London, built on a 12hp chassis. A two-seater, it had an early form of the rumble or dickey seat popular in later years, in this case a single chair that hinged out for its intrepid occupant. With no safety belt it could be easy for three to start a journey and only two finish it.

The Benz 16/40hp model of 1912 to 1914 fitted with a 3969cc four-cylinder engine running up to 1,600 rpm and some 70 mph. Four-seater touring body in a style that would continue postwar but with improved headlight mounting. The side lights were very neat.

After 1908 motor racing stagnated in Europe but boomed in the USA until 1912 when the French Grand Prix was run once again. The USA then turned to the Indianapolis 500, first run in 1911, and the Grand Prix de l'Automobile Club de France was run on July 4th, 1914, at Lyons. It was a clean sweep for Mercedes with Christian Lautenschlager the winner.

This 1914 Benz was used by L.J. Wellard to complete a rally from John O' Groats to Land's End held during 1975 after his 1913 Renault had some problems.

An early Benz from 1914 at a later-day rally with its hood up to keep the weather at bay. The box on the running board was typical of the time and contained either the battery or tools. Neat side lights on the scuttle in addition to those fitted below the headlights.

Mercedes entered five cars for the 1914 French Grand Prix with this one driven by their Belgian agent, Théodore Pilette who had finished third in a race on the Sarth circuit at Le Mans in 1913. He was out of luck for the next year and retired with a broken propeller shaft on lap four.

Max Sailer led the 1914 French Grand Prix from the start, forcing the Peugeot cars to the limit in their attempt to keep up. On the sixth lap the Mercedes engine failed but in the end the leading Peugeot broke a valve and Mercedes finished first, second and third with Sailer having set the fastest lap.

Louis Wagner finished second to Lautenschlager in the 1914 French Grand Prix with Otto Salzer third. All three were just too good for the Peugeot driven by Boillot, who was seldom beaten, and his engine expired on the last lap when he lay second. A month later Europe was at war.

A Benz from 1914 in royal use in Sweden where it carried the King, Gustavus V, hence the crown mounted on the top of the radiator. Tram lines and stone setts or cobbles were the normal road surface in towns at that time.

A Mercedes 90 built in 1913 with a Corsica body but seen here many years later. Each of the four exhaust pipes was enclosed by metal hose and this feature would continue to be used up to the late-1930s. Still chain drive and rear brakes only on this model.

The team line up of cars, drivers and mechanics for the 1914 French Grand Prix run just a month before the Great War began. From the right they were driven by Salzer who was third, Sailer who set the fastest lap before retiring, Wagner who was second and Lautenschlager who won. On the end, the fifth car was driven by Pilette, the Mercedes Belgium agent.

A Mercedes-Cardan-Wagen from 1916, built using a 28/60hp, four-cylinder engine with shaft drive to the rear wheels. Twin boxes on the running board for battery or tools and some weather protection for the rear-seat occupants. From 1914 to 1918 Mercedes built several thousand cars as well as trucks and buses.

This 1916 Mercedes 16/50hp model was fitted with a Knight sleeve-valve engine. The firm used this type from 1910 to 1924 as an alternative to the poppet valve as they were very quiet and smooth in operation. However, they were slow-running engines of limited power that were prone to wear and seizure as well as producing clouds of oil smoke in the exhaust.

Left: This Mercedes-Wagen of 1916-17 was also referred to as the Kaiser-Jagdwagen and therefore carried the royal crest of the German leader on the rear door panel. There was a second windscreen and folding hood to protect him and his passenger from the weather.

Count Zborowski in the 21.5-litre Benz he drove at Brooklands in 1922. A monster car from an earlier age, it was typical of the type the Count drove at the track, but was too difficult to hold on the bumpy concrete bankings of the motor course to be competitive.

It may have been the roaring twenties but this fine 1922 Mercedes limousine hardly fitted that scene. A 6/25hp model with shaft drive, its style had moved on from prewar although it still lacked front-wheel brakes. A speaking tube close to the driver's head enabled instructions to be conveyed to him.

In the heady postwar era Paul Daimler introduced supercharged models that were fast and glamorous, having used this type in the 1922 Targa Florio. This picture shows the affluent and fashionable market that Mercedes sought, but even in the USA this had its limits.

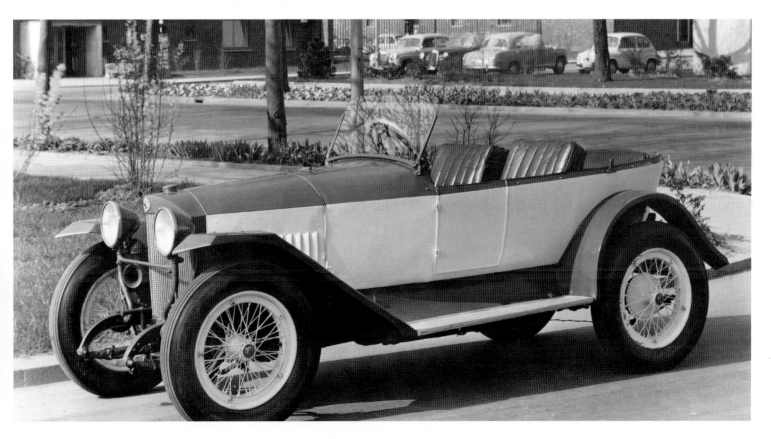

A modern day picture of a 1918 Benz, said to be a 6/18hp model for sport and racing. This might explain the offset of the two seats but reality suggests that this car is more of an open tourer.

Famous photograph of Count Giulio Masetti on his way to winning the 1922 Targa Florio in his privately entered Mercedes that was one of the 1914 Grand Prix cars. Two others were entered, driven by Lautenschlager and Salzer, plus two 28/95 cars, one of which was supercharged. There were also two 1.5-litre four-cylinder cars that had twin overhead camshafts, four valves per cylinder, and a supercharger that fed air into the carburettor and could be engaged or not as required. This was a system the firm used for many years.

Early-1920s Mercedes-Knight 16/45 model with the sleeve-valve engine that gave it smoothness, silence and low-speed pulling but wear problems and high oil consumption. It was an efficient but low speed engine type that fell from favour as the poppet valve improved.

One of the 1.5-litre, four-cylinder, 16-valve, twin-cam supercharged cars entered by Mercedes in the 1922 Targa Florio and driven by Paul Sheef. The blower could be engaged by the driver and raised the power from 54 to 82 bhp but the tight Sicilian circuit inhibited its use while the German drivers had limited knowledge of the long and tortuous course. Sheef finished 20th and the other car retired.

A Benz for touring and sports use with a four-seater open body and furled hood. Built from 1921 to 1925, it had a 16/50hp, six-cylinder engine and the solid Benz reputation for producing well-built cars. This was a real asset in the days of hyper-inflation in Germany.

In 1923 Ferdinand Porsche joined Daimler in Stuttgart to improve the supercharged cars further. This was the result that won the 1924 Targa Florio with Christian Werner at the wheel and was powered by a 1986cc four-cylinder engine with twin-overhead camshafts opening four valves per cylinder.

The remarkable Benz Tropfenwagen, or tear-drop car, that was based on a design by Dr. Edmund Rumpler and completed by Benz engineers working under Max Wagner. It reflected modern thinking with the engine mounted behind the driver with the gearbox and rear axle in one with it. In this form a radiator sat in front of the engine and protruded into the airstream under a cowl, believed to be for oil cooling.

The Tropfenwagen minus the body to show the fuel tank at the front, extensively-lightened chassis, and the 2-litre, twin-cam, six-cylinder engine. The car was only raced once, at Monza in 1923, when Fernando Minoia finished fourth and Hörner was fifth. Versions with two seats, headlights and wings were also built for road use.

Engine and transmission of the Tropfenwagen with the radiator fitted above the gearbox, curved to match the body shape, and with a small header tank that sat out in the wind so was streamlined. Suspension was by a beam axle and quarter-elliptic leaf springs at the front but by independent swing axle at the rear with the same spring type.

Christian Werner during a pit stop, possibly the lengthy one that nearly cost him the 1924 Targa Florio. In the race he was accompanied by Karl Sailer while other Mercedes cars were driven by Christian Lautenschlager and Alfred Neubauer, later to be famous as the Mercedes-Benz team manager before and after the war.

The mighty Mercedes 24/100/140 model of 1924 with a 6.0-litre, six-cylinder engine with supercharger that was clutch driven from the engine when the driver opened the throttle fully. The supercharger then blew air into the carburettor in the manner used by Mercedes for many years. This car had a landaulette body but other forms were used.

In postwar Sweden the royal house switched from Benz to this 24/100hp Mercedes of 1924, the 6.0-litre, six-cylinder engine without the supercharger. A limousine body with the crown carried ahead of the radiator and a high degree of polish as would be expected.

The more sporting 1924 version of the 24/100/140 model with its six litres and six cylinders with blower to urge the four-seater touring body along. Four-wheel brakes had appeared by then and were needed to cope with the speed and weight, even though the K-version (K for Kurz or short) had a shorter wheelbase.

The Italian Grand Prix held at Monza in October, 1924, was a sad day for Mercedes. They entered a team of 2.0-litre cars with blown straight-eight engines that produced 170 bhp at 7,000 rpm. Designed by Porsche, they were fast but handled poorly and Count Zborowski, seen here refuelling, crashed and was killed. In respect, the cars driven by Werner and Neubauer were withdrawn, Masetti having already retired.

The 1925 Mercedes 2.0-litre racing car with the straight-eight engine in which Rudolf Caracciola won the first German Grand Prix held at the Avus in 1926. The other Mercedes crashed in the wet event, but Caracciola thrived in the conditions and became known as the Regenmeister, or rain master.

Right: Not long before the two firms amalgamated, Mercedes offered this 12/40hp supercharged model and this example had a neat Compton two-seater coupé body with dickey seat fitted to it, but had to manage with rear brakes only.

Left: Inspecting the engine of a 1925 Mercedes 33/140hp model with the short chassis wheelbase. The features of the room and the left-hand drive suggest the USA although the lady is hardly a 1920s flapper.

In 1926 Mercedes and Benz joined forces for their mutual benefit and the firm became Daimler-Benz. Neither could expect to survive alone and it took time for the new combination to function well. This Mercedes model K was typical of the result, a replacement for the 28/95 that ran on with the new name.

By 1928 Mercedes-Benz had settled down, reduced its labour force and begun to adopt some mass-production methods. Glamour came from the expensive sports cars but it was models such as this six-cylinder Stuttgart saloon that formed the backbone of sales. After a hesitant start it sold well for many years with a variety of body styles.

Ferdinand Porsche created the Mercedes-Benz S-type in 1927 with a 6.8-litre, six-cylinder, overhead-camshaft engine and from it came the SS Super Sports and the SSK Super Sports Kurz, or short, these two with a 7.1-litre engine. Fabulous cars built in small numbers and expensive. The radiator cap, surmounted by the star, included a thermometer.

The 24/100/140 six continued on as the four-seater tourer and this example had an open body by Erdmann & Rossi of Berlin. A good car for four to travel in comfort with their luggage on the rear rack as was then common.

This 1926 Stuttgart was far from home when it took part in the Statesman Rally held in Calcutta. On the day it had to be push-started every time it set off, maybe its number 13 being an ill-omen. The snake horn and carriage lamps by the scuttle were most likely to be local additions.

A 1926 Mercedes Type K with six-cylinder 6.2-litre engine rated as 24/110/160hp, the last when the blower was in use. The body was by von Saoutchik, one of the many who supplied coachwork for Mercedes-Benz cars in the period between the wars, and a saloon in this instance.

The Nürburgring was opened in 1927 with Caracciola winning the first race and Otto Merz the German Grand Prix a month later, both driving Mercedes cars. For 1928 the Grand Prix was for sports cars and the first three places went to the firm, the cars seen here leaving the start.

The Nürburg was another good, solid Mercedes-Benz that was built for a decade after this 1928 saloon appeared as the 18/80. It used a 4.6-litre, eight-cylinder, side-valve engine, so catered for a different market to the Stuttgart, and had a variety of bodies, most the saloon type.

Finish of the 1928 German Grand Prix held at the Nürburgring and run for sports cars. Caracciola won with assistance from Werner whose car finished third after he had handed it over to Willy Walb while Otto Merz came second, driving alone for the entire race.

A fine example of the touring S-type with its hood up. Classic Mercedes exhaust pipes from the six-cylinder engine and a big, heavy car able to reach 100 mph although hard pressed to stop quickly from that speed.

The large K-type from around 1928 with its 6.2-litre, overhead-camshaft, six-cylinder engine, the model also listed as the 24/110/160hp. This example had a fine six-light saloon body by Farina with the luggage mounted at the rear in the fashion of the day.

Less exotic than the sports models but much more popular, the Stuttgart 10/50hp model with its 2.6-litre, six-cylinder, side-valve engine, three speeds, artillery wheels and flat radiator. Built from 1928 in this cabriolet form as well as saloon, roadster and tourer.

The Super Sports Kurz Mercedes-Benz with its short chassis, external exhausts, cycle wings, quick-action radiator cap, low build, blown engine, aero-screens behind the fold-flat windscreen, all added up to charisma. And then there was the SSKL, the leicht or light version with drilled chassis and raced by the factory.

This 1928 S-type had an open tourer body by Freestone & Webb of London and was first registered in that city. A large storage box was incorporated into the running board and the split windscreen could be partly opened in poor weather.

This S-type was listed in Britain as the 36/220hp and was built in 1929. Here, it was on the line at Syston Park and ready for a timed run that started the clock when the front wheel ran over the hockey-stick timer that had to be pulled away before the rear wheel arrived.

Line drawing of the 1929 Nürburg six-light Pullmann-limousine that was the top of that series. The saloon was similar, seating six or seven, and a tourer for the same seating or four to five was an option along with a sports coupé.

A 1929 Type-S cabriolet somewhere in postwar Britain when petrol was 5/10d for premium-grade petrol and the garage offered no shelter as you filled up. A sign indicates that they carried out the annual tests that had been introduced for older vehicles, at first for those of ten years or more, now three.

The 24/100/140 model was also known as the 630 and built first as a Mercedes. This 1929 example had the Benz name added and became the K-type. Large, sober in appearance but still with the sporting pointed radiator with a star on each side. In this case windscreen wipers were fitted, a real improvement over the split screen that remained for many.

Fine Super Sports from 1929 with a fixed-head coupé body at the far end of a very long bonnet. Firms such as Corsica, Freestone & Webb, Castagna and Saoutchik all supplied bodies and all were attractive and impressive.

Left: In 1951 a Midnight Concours was held in Eastbourne on the south coast of England and one of the entries was this 1929 S-type 36/220hp Mercedes-Benz. A black tie and evening dress affair with the car driver and passenger dressed to suit the occasion and to match their car.

Grosser Mercedes Reihen 8 Zylinder 150/200 PS   1105

In 1930 Mercedes-Benz introduced the 770 Grosser series powered by an eight-cylinder, overhead-valve, 7603cc engine with a supercharger an option. Big in every sense, the series would in time become the car for heads of state and the Reich Chancellery.

This 1930 Grosser 770 was fitted with a coupé body that was fixed over the rear compartment but could be open over the front seats. A division went between front and rear seat while the pointed radiator and external exhaust pipes continued. The front plate says 'Estado Miranda'.

This 1930 example of the Grosser 770 had the supercharger fitted so was also listed as 30/150/200hp from its eight cylinders and 7.6-litre. The four-seater cabriolet body has the top folded down and carries a flag pennant staff by the right headlight.

For this picture the cabriolet body had the top raised and the windows wound up. It also had a cover for the spare wheel and was listed as the D cabriolet, there being types B, C and F as well. All large and all quite conventional as regards engine and chassis.

This was the 1952 Brighton Speed Trials held on the Madeira Drive by the sea shore with a 1930 Super Sports model on the start line making ready for its run over the standing-start kilometer.

Fine study of a Super Sports model with right-hand drive and the spare wheel on the same side in this case. They also went on the left and some cars had two. A cabriolet body behind the tall radiator, wire wheels and expensive then or now.

The 350 Mannheim introduced in 1929 as a mid-range model between the Stuttgart and Nürburg became the 370 in the same year with a 3.7-litre, six-cylinder, side-valve engine. In 1931 the prosaic saloon was joined by this Sport model that had a shorter wheelbase and cabriolet body.

The car happens to be a Super Sports from the late-1920s, but what else better to have a Lalique mascot on its radiator cap to go with the two triple-note horns, extra lights and the Mercedes-Benz insignia mounted high on each wing.

This 1931 Grosser limousine was the property of the Emperor of Japan, Hirohito, hence the chrysanthemum on the radiator that was repeated on the small lights on the roof corners. Professor Hama stands by the car, a type also used by ex-Kaiser Wilhelm II.

Staid, even boring, but the model for the successful man who could ride in the rear of this 1932 Nürburg Pullmann-limousine concentrating on his papers while the chauffeur did the driving. A conventional car for that type of mind.

The 170 was introduced for 1932 to suit the economic conditions of the times with a 1.7-litre, six-cylinder, side-valve engine, two or four-door saloon body at first, and a price well below that of the Stuttgart. While conventional on the surface it had independent suspension all round and proved to be a popular model.

Left: A car with presence as well as style in the German manner set off by the cabriolet A body on a 1932 Super Sports model. With seven litres, six cylinders and the supercharger, its 200 bhp could push it along at over 110 mph, despite its size.

This Nürburg was from around 1934 and is seen at a Butlins Holiday Camp at Bognor during a 1963 rally. It had the four to five seater touring body and was a sound and durable model.

The 290 model with a 2.9-litre, six-cylinder, side-valve engine replaced the 200 Stuttgart for 1934, continuing the same theme with an extensive range of saloon and cabriolet bodies. This is the D-type with four seats, four doors and wire wheels.

The supercharged line took a new form in 1933 with the 380K that had a 3.8-litre, straight-eight, overhead-valve engine. Saloon, cabriolet, coupé and roadster bodies were built and all rode on independent suspension front and rear, but were only offered for two years, this the saloon.

Der neue MERCEDES-BENZ Typ 200, 2 Liter, 6 Zylinder, 40 PS,
mit Schwingachsen, 4-sitzige Limousine.

The 200 was revised for 1933 and while it kept the well established side-valve six engine, it gained all-round indepedent suspension. A host of bodies were listed with saloon, tourer, roadster, cabriolet and limousine.

The largest body fitted to the 200 built from 1933 to 1936 was this six-light Pullmann limousine. A large car that must have overwhelmed the 2-litre engine so it was hard pressed to reach 60 mph, but did travel quietly and with dignity.

The 380K was joined and then replaced by the 500K during 1934. The new model followed the same format with the engine stretched out to 5.0-litre but installed on a longer wheelbase and with a host of body styles offered, including this streamlined saloon for autobahn travel. Not as stark as the SSK of the late-1920s, the model was a classic for its time.

Mercedes-Benz returned to grand prix racing in 1934 with their W25 built to suit the new 750 kg formula. Highly advanced and part funded by the Reich, as was Auto Union, the W25 had a 3364cc, straight-eight engine with twin-overhead camshafts, 32 valves and a supercharger. The four-speed gearbox was built in unit with the rear axle and all four wheels had independent suspension and hydraulically-operated drum brakes. It was soon stretched to 3710cc and won first time out at the Eifelrennen and later in Italy and Spain.

The 130H was a totally different model that appeared in 1934 with its 1.3-litre, four-cylinder, side-valve engine mouned behind the rear axle along with the gearbox. There was all-round independent suspension and a backbone chassis but it was not a success in either saloon or cabriolet form.

From the 130H came this 150H in 1935 with its 1.5-litre engine moved forward to be in front of the rear axle. The sporting roadster body certainly caught the eye with three headlights and a spare wheel on each side, but the handling was poor and both it and the 130H were replaced by the 170H in 1936.

Left: More streamlining, including a cowl, was used for record breaking attempts and at the 1935 Avus race. By then the engine capacity had increased to 3992cc and rose further to 4309cc for some cars at the end of the season. Here at the Avus, Caracciola was receiving instructions from Neubauer during practice but drove an open car in the race in which he won his heat but retired from the final.

Gottlieb Daimler was born in 1834 in the middle house of this group in the town of Württemberg, and his first and only motorcycle stands on the left, abandoned as soon as it had proved that his engine worked. The car is a 1934 Mercedes-Benz 380K, the first of the new series of supercharged sports models of that decade.

Taken at the 1934 French Grand Prix where Mercedes-Benz entered three cars but had all of them retire as did the Auto Union entries to leave the race to Alfa Romeo. It did not take the German teams long to rectify their problems and begin their total domination of grand prix racing.

Mercedes-Benz and Auto Union were expected to go record breaking as well as to win grand prix and one result was additional streamlining. This is the modified W25 with the 3992cc engine developing 430 bhp at 5,800 rpm and used by Rudolf Caracciola to attack the mile standing-start record on the road at Gyon near Budapest in Hungary late in 1934. No front brakes and no louvres in the bonnet or sides were all part of the careful preparation for a specific task.

In 1936 the rear-engined car became the 170H with a 1.7-litre engine that continued with the backbone chassis and all-round independent suspension. As well as this saloon there was a version with a soft roof that could be rolled back but neither was a success so they were dropped after 1938.

This is what Mercedes-Benz meant to enthusiasts in the mid-1930s, a large open car with a supercharged engine, in this case the 500K of 1935 in touring form but able to reach 100 mph.

Right: The old box form of the 170 of 1931 was replaced in 1936 by the 170V that had a more modern style. Unlike the 170H it kept the engine at the front but had the backbone chassis and independent suspension while a variety of bodies were used, this two-door saloon the most basic.

Mercédès-Benz „Type 500" à compresseur. Roadster
Mercedes-Benz „Type 500" with supercharger. Roadster
Mercedes-Benz „Typ 500" mit Kompressor. Roadster

The roadster version of the 500K with its big 5-litre blown eight engine pushing out 160 bhp with the supercharger engaged and 100 bhp without it. Tremendous style from the sweeping wings to the spare wheel on the tail and always an expensive motor car.

It is said that this 500K was made for Barbara Hutton in 1936. It carries a British registration number issued in London around that time but this could have been bought to suit her initials.

Short version of the streamlined saloon body for a 500K of 1936. In this case only two exhausts for the eight cylinders, no window behind the door but still with the rear-wheel spats to enhance the style. All these models have attractive lines in one way or another.

Mercedes-Benz Typ 260 D. Pullman-Limousine mit Dieselmotor, 6 Sitze.
Mercédès-Benz Type 260 D. Limousine Pullman, Moteur Diesel, 6 places.
Mercedes-Benz Type 260 D. Pullman-Limousine, Diesel engine, 6 seater.
Mercedes-Benz Werkphoto (39)

Bestellnummer:

31054

In 1936 the firm introduced the 260D that was based on their existing practice with all-round independent suspension but was fitted with a 2.5-litre diesel engine, the first production car to do this. It had four cylinders and overhead valves but its modest 45 bhp was hardly enough to push its considerable weight along, especially in this Pullmann-limousine form.

MERCEDES-BENZ Heckmotorwagen Typ 170 H, Cabrio-Limousine, 4-5 Sitze
MERCEDES-BENZ Type 170 H, à moteur arrière, Cabrio-Limousine, 4-5 places
MERCEDES-BENZ Type 170 H, with rear engine, Cabrio-Limousine, 4-5 seater
Mercedes-Benz Werkphoto (38)

Bestellnummer:

29040a

The rear-engined 170H suffered from having a heavy, cast-iron, water-cooled engine hung at the rear so its handling was inevitably poor. In addition to the saloon, this cabriolet was offered with a fabric top panel that could be rolled away.

The 770 Grosser model with supercharger was a firm favourite of the Nazi party leaders who could enjoy its splendour from the rear seat. Field-Marshal Goering was no exception and is seen here after a sunny ride with the top down.

Another of the late-1930s models was the 320 introduced in 1937 with a 3.2-litre, six-cylinder, side-valve engine, later increased to 3.4-litre, that had to haul rather too much weight along. It was built with various body styles, this the cabriolet D that seated five, and had hydraulic brakes to help stop it.

By 1937 the W25 had been replaced by the W125 that had a 5663cc eight-cylinder engine with twin-overhead camshafts and four valves per cylinder. For the very fast Avus track it was fitted with a fully-streamlined body that included wheel covers, from which this record breaker was evolved. It was powered by a 5577cc V-12 engine and Caracciola used it to set a record at 268.7 mph in January 1938.

After the 500K came the 540K with its larger engine, 180 bhp and even greater fuel consumption. As with the earlier models, there were many factory bodies plus customs, this the rather sedate and Teutonic saloon to carry four or five.

Wheeling out the W125, the car that won many of the 1937 grand prix races with drivers Caracciola, Lang and von Brauchitsch at the wheel. Under the streamlining went a frame constructed from oval-section tubing with independent front suspension by wishbones and coil springs, and De Dion at the rear by torsion bars. The four-speed gearbox was built in unit with the rear axle and massive 400mm drum brakes were used.

The 5663cc eight-cylinder engine of the 1937 W125 was a twin-cam, 32-valve unit that continued with the pre-Great War practice of having forged-steel cylinders with the ports and water jackets welded in place. They were built in blocks of four cylinders with the supercharger at the front of the engine and if any slight leak developed, the firm had a welder flown out to the race circuit to seal it.

The 170V model was the most common prewar car from the firm and one body form listed was the roadster for two, with two more able to use the rumble seat. This modest, reliable car would continue in the range right on to 1955.

The streamlined body developed for the fast grand prix circuits was also used for record attempts in 1937 and 1938. For these it ran with wheel spats in place, the driver nearly fully enclosed and a smaller air entry slot at the front.

Taken during the British Grand Prix held at Donington Park late in 1937, and thus the last race run to the 750 kg formula, with Manfred von Brauchitsch in the pits for fuel and tyres. He finished second to Bernd Rosemeyer's Auto Union and they shared the fastest lap while Caracciola brought a second W125 home in third place.

Two of the streamlined cars minus wheel spats, and an Auto Union, during the 1937 Avus race in which von Brauchitsch, in car 36, won heat two but retired in the final won by Hermann Lang in car 37. The leading car had the 5577cc V-12 engine first conceived for the W25 but found to be too heavy. Even when lightened it still put too much weight on the front wheels so was only suited to high-speed events.

The streamlined Mercedes on the Frankfurt-Darmstadt autobahn for testing without front wheel spats or rear wheel fairings. The square hatch gave access to the engine and test runs were made late in 1936 using the V-12 engine.

The Avusrennen of 1937 was run on a circuit comprising two six-mile straights joined at each end, one of which was banked that year. This allowed the lap record to rise from 162 to 173 mph and saw both German teams running fully streamlined cars. This is Caracciola who won heat one but retired in the final; his car fitted with spats on the front wheels but not the rears.

Alfred Neubauer flagging Caracciola away in his 1937 W125, either on a standing-start record attempt or a hill climb. For the latter the brakes would be reduced in width to lighten them, while for the former the front brakes were usually dispensed with.

The W125 of Manfred von Brauchitsch being pushed onto the grid for the 1937 British Grand Prix in which it finished second. Behind is the ERA driven by Arthur Dobson who was eighth but not classified as a finisher along with the other non-German cars that were all outside the time limit.

Caracciola climbing into the streamlined W125 he drove at the Avus in 1937, its last year of use. After winning the first heat he was forced out of the final with back axle trouble.

A popular, mid-range model for the late-1930s was this 230 that was listed with saloon, cabriolet, tourer and limousine bodies, the last two on a longer chassis with independent front suspension. The shorter chassis had a backbone frame and all-round independent suspension.

Alfred Neubauer making a point to Max Sailer, with flat cap, as they discuss the streamlined W125 driven by von Brauchitsch in the 1937 Avus race. The car was fitted with the V-12 engine whose extra weight on the front wheels suited the fast circuit. Mercedes tool boxes were shaped to sit on the body without moving.

Dick Seaman in his W125 during the 1937 British Grand Prix at Donington. He was unlucky in that an Auto Union rammed him on the opening lap which damaged his rear suspension and this later forced his retirement.

For the upper end of the market that did not wish for a Grosser there was the 320 listed with the usual choice of body styles including this four-to-five seater cabriolet. It still had the side-valve, six-cylinder engine and was no lightweight so it took its time to reach its 80 mph and the hydraulic brakes were a real asset and had to work hard to earn their keep.

Rudolf Caracciola exiting one of the corners of the tight Donington Park circuit during the 1937 British Grand Prix on his way to third place in his W125. Behind him is B. Bira in a Maserati who came sixth, the first car behind the German teams but not classified as a finisher, being outside the time limit.

The interesting, rear-engined 170H as for 1937 in its two-door saloon form. It had poor handling due to the engine weight on the rear wheels so was a slow seller. The central spot light was an interesting styling feature found both before and after the war on other marques and models.

By 1938 the firm was well into production of vehicles for the Wehrmacht using their car, racing and truck expertise. This example was the G5 colonial and pursuit car that had both four-wheel drive and four-wheel steering.

For 1938, grand prix cars were limited to 3.0-litre if supercharged and had to weigh 850 kg with wheels and tyres. For this the firm built the W154 fitted with a V-12, quad-cam, 48-valve engine with twin superchargers. This drove a five-speed gearbox and was installed in a chassis developed from the W125 while the body was lower but wider.

A 1938 four-door 230 saloon on London plates and in need of a clean. The cross-roads were at Upper Swell and the Donnington Brewery had nothing to do with the racing circuit for it was in Gloucestershire on minor roads, hence their poor condition.

This 540K from 1938 was the top end of the sporting range that year, in this case with one of the three cabriolet bodies. There was 180 bhp under the bonnet and a prodigious thirst for fuel but this was of little concern to those who could afford this expensive model.

Another 230 for 1938, in this case fitted with the convertible coupé body that was conservative in line and rather heavy for the side-valve engine to haul along so acceleration was a gentle and leisurely process.

Taken at the 1938 Berlin Motor Show with a 540K Roadster showing off its fine lines, external exhaust pipes and raked, split windscreen. Only for the wealthy, for the rest it would be something more modest such as the 170V until postwar and the VW.

A G5 in deep mud and demonstrating the advantage of four-wheel drive for any off-road work providing the right tyres were fitted. Not the vehicle for speed and hardly cheap to build or run and service, but well suited to its tasks.

Dick Seaman at the Melbourne Corner on the extended Donington Park race circuit during the 1938 British Grand Prix in which he finished third. The cars dropped down the hill to this hairpin and when they climbed back to the finish usually left the road at the summit.

The 1938 Grosser 770K had a new chassis with all-round independent suspension based on that of the 540K. The same 7.7-litre, eight-cylinder engine was used with the supercharger fitted as standard as were hydraulic brakes. Much favoured in this cabriolet form for German staff officers in postwar films of the Second World War

Mercedes-Benz Typ 540 mit Kompressor, Offener Tourenwagen, 4-5 Sitze. Sonderausführung
mit Windschutzscheibe für den Fond.
Mercédès-Benz Type 540 à compresseur, Torpédo, 4-5 places. Construction particulière
avec pare-brise pour lefond.
Mercedes-Benz Type 540 with supercharger, Touring car, 4-5 seater. Special design
with wind-screen for the back seat.

27752

Mercedes-Benz Werkphoto (37)

Another body style used on the 540K model in the late-1930s was this four to five seater touring type that was a special design with a second windscreen for the rear seats.

Hermann Lang had been a Mercedes mechanic, was allowed to practice in the 1935 Monaco race and joined the team the following year. He won the first major race of 1937, the Tripoli Grand Prix, and won it again in 1938 driving this W154 before going on to a very successful season in 1939.

Generals and ranks above only need apply for this 1938 Grosser 770K complete with Nazi pennants and extra lights. A big, heavy cabriolet, but well able to cover an autobahn at high speed until more fuel was required.

Another cabriolet body style used for the 540K in 1938 with seating for two or three who could travel far and fast in great comfort and style. The handling was best not pushed too far and it was thirsty, but had good hydraulic brakes and a fine line to set heads turning.

Wonderful lines, great presence and a car to dominate the roads meant a 770K Grosser Mercedes-Benz. The two-door cabriolet body with top down offered the populace a brief glimpse of the great in passing plus the pleasure of the chauffeur opening the door and hinging a seat forward for the owner to step forth.

Ferdinand Porsche was responsible for this car, known as the T80, that was built to attack the land speed record. This stood at 369.7 mph late in 1939, the same car reaching 394.2 mph in 1947, and the T80 was planned to exceed 400 mph. The side wings were to provide down force and stability but the car never ran.

MERCEDES-BENZ Typ 540 mit Kompressor, Spezial-Roadster, 2 Sitze
MERCEDES-BENZ Type 540 à compresseur, Roadster, 2 places
MERCEDES-BENZ Type 540 with supercharger, Roadster, 2 seater

Mercedes Benz-Werkphoto (37)

Bestellnummer:

24187

A great deal of very expensive, very powerful and very thirsty car for just two people summed up the sports roadster 540K, in this case with the hood raised. No question of a rumble seat with a 100 mph plus potential, but definitely a car to cause a stir as it drew up at the hotel steps.

At the other end of the scale there was the 170V sports roadster built in much larger numbers with a modest performance from its four side-valve cylinders. Reliable and affordable with a Teutonic style, but 100 km/h rather than mph, and a lot less fuel.

The T80 had a 44.5-litre V-12 engine just behind the driver who sat well forward between the front wheels. There were four rear wheels, all of them driven, and the hand made body fitted to the tubular framework over a great deal of complexity in all areas. In order that the car could attempt the record in Germany, rather than the salt flats at Bonneville in the USA, the new autobahn near Dessau was built with both carriageways in one without a central grass strip and finished to a high standard.

Mercedes-Benz went record breaking early in 1939 using a fully streamlined car with a 3-litre engine installed. Caracciola was the driver and the autobahn near Dessau the place for the attempt that produced new class records for the standing and flying start mile and kilometer, the fastest at over 248 mph.

The firm produced a range of commercial road vehicles and some of them were based on car models, this 170V light van being a typical example. A steady plodder rather than a race horse, it was well suited to its tasks of local work carrying goods or equipment.

An older model from the mid-1930s with a more upright radiator and either a 170 or 200, both of which had six-cylinder, side-valve engines of 1692 and 1962cc respectively. Seen here postwar having covered many kilometers but still fit and able to cover many more and do its job, just as always.

In 1939 the Tripoli Grand Prix was run for 1.5-litre voiturette cars in a bid to keep the German teams away from this well-rewarded event. To the consternation of the Italians, Mercedes-Benz turned up with two W165 cars powered by V-8 engines and proceeded to finish first and second in the only race they ran in.

This 1939 540K had a Freestone & Webb body fitted to it and in the process lost most of its German lines to take on British ones. However, the radiator star, external spare wheel and detail of the petrol filler cap all spoke of its origins.

One of the special bodies fitted to a 540K in 1939 was this fixed-head coupé. More Italian than German, with the extra, central headlight, flowing lines and the radiator star replaced by a transfer on the car nose.

Truly Teutonic in its size and grandeur with long bonnet, sumptuous seats and substantial hood. A 1939 Grosser 770K with five-seater cabriolet D body that retained the pointed radiator from the distant past.

The start of the 1939 Tripoli Grand Prix with Lang already ahead of Caracciola and the rest of the field of Alfa Romeo and Maserati cars that would finish far astern. Lang won for the third year in succession and set the fastest lap at over 133 mph in the process while Caracciola finished four minutes ahead of the third man.

Side view of the 1939 540K fitted with a special two-door, two-seater coupé body. Built for speed so there were few extraneous protrusions from the body other than the side lights, even the door handles being recessed into it.

Hermann Lang crossing the finishing line at the 1939 Tripoli Grand Prix for his third win in succession. A state lottery was run in conjunction with this race so the prize money was very good and the Italians had tired of German cars winning this, hence the sudden change to 1.5-litre for 1939 which made no difference.

Dick Seaman during the 1938 British Grand Prix in which he finished third after losing a lap when his car spun on oil dropped by another. Several other drivers had similar excitements, including Nuvolari who went on to win the race for Auto Union.

A 540K cabriolet A from 1939 at the end of an era of such cars that came with all manner of bodies but were always large, fast, thirsty, extravagant and most impressive.

Right: The Yugoslav Grand Prix run at Belgrade on the 3rd September, 1939, was the last race run to the 3-litre formula. Manfred von Brauchitsch finished second after a spin and his car was the W163 the firm used that year, it being the final development of the V-12 and having two-stage supercharging among its improvements from the W154 of 1938.

Left: The engine of the 1.5-litre W165 run at Tripoli in 1939 after earlier trials at the Nürburgring. A V-8, each bank of cylinders had twin-overhead camshafts, and it was supercharged using all the tried and tested race knowledge of the firm. The power output was 256 bhp at 8,000 rpm which was more than sufficient in 1939 although the Alfa Romeo 158 had exceeded this by 1948.

The personal parade 770K made in 1942 for Hitler. With his personal flag up front it was no surprise to find bullet-proof tyres and windows, considerable armour-plating, a 300-litre fuel tank and a 400hp engine to haul it all along. However, his seat was raised for a better sight of the Fuehrer.

While one of the prewar models had to make do postwar, the firm was never idle and by 1951 had the 220 series in production with a 2.2-litre, overhead-camshaft, six-cylinder engine. The prewar line remained, although with the headlights set into the wings, and saloon, fixed-head coupé, and two or four seat cabriolet bodies were used.

During the war the 170V was modified to run using this gas producer system whose presence on the rear bumper moved the spare wheel onto the roof. Most countries had to adopt such methods to keep their vehicles running at all.

An early postwar variant of the 170V built for the police to use to move men about. The prewar side-valve engine was stretched to 1767cc and an overhead-valve diesel version was also built, both slow, heavy but very reliable, something the times demanded.

The first of the 300 Series appeared in 1951 to take the firm back to the more prestigious sector of the market. A 3.0-litre, six-cylinder, overhead-camshaft engine propelled the four-door saloon able to carry five or six in comfort, style and speed.

The 220S used the same engine as the saloon, but had more power, and was available with a four-seater coupé or a cabriolet body with just two doors and a stiffened construction to compensate for the lack of a roof.

This 220S was fitted with the cabriolet body built to carry two or three people rather than four or five. With the top raised it offered a snug ride out of the weather.

From 1952 the 300S was available in roadster, coupé and this cabriolet form based on a shortened saloon chassis and using the same engine. There was also a four-door 300 cabriolet, both built in small numbers and fine cars although soon to be supplanted by the 300SL.

Mercedes-Benz returned to Le Mans in 1952 and ran out first and second after the leading Talbot broke a rod just 75 minutes from the end when four laps ahead. Hermann Lang and Fritz Riess were the winners and one Mercedes tried an air brake fitted to its roof during practice. The car was the 300SL with the gullwing doors.

The 300SL, or Sports Light, in its W194 form for 1952 and as run at Le Mans. The engine was canted well over to keep the height down and its weight, plus that of the transmission, was offset by panelling the body in aluminium. Most cars were built in coupé form with the gullwing doors brought about by the deep sides of the tubular chassis, but some open versions were built for other 1952 races.

The 300S Roadster from 1952 was one of several body styles offered on the shortened 300 saloon chassis, the others being the coupé and cabriolet. All shared the same 3.0-litre, single-cam, six-cylinder engine and offered speedy motoring.

For 1954 the firm introduced the 180 with a monocoque body structure to replace the elderly 170. The new model kept the old side-valve engine at first but gained a better one in time, also being built with diesel engines to become the company base model.

The 170 soldiered on to 1955 in SV and SD forms, the latter the diesel-powered model, and all with their prewar style to the end. Never exciting but a car that served the firm and owners well through some difficult times.

The driving compartment of the 300SL of 1952 when it was first seen. The very wide door sills concealed part of the complex chassis structure while the engine installation ensured that only left-hand-drive cars could be built. The full instrumentation included shrouded speedometer and rev-counter dials, plus a chronometer at centre.

Another form of the 170SD was this diesel-powered service van used by the company in Britain. This was slow and certain but for the grand prix cars they had a transporter based in part on the 300SL and able to carry a W196 racing car on its back at up to 100 mph.

Well-known actor, James Robertson-Justice in a 300SL from 1957, its last year of production. Under the bonnet went a 3.0-litre, six-cylinder, overhead-camshaft engine with fuel injection and dry-sump lubrication, the assembly laid over in the tubular, space frame chassis. A small number were built with an aluminium body while all have the side vents.

Juan Fangio on his way to winning the 1954 French Grand Prix to mark the firm's return to racing. Karl Kling was second, one-tenth of a second adrift, while Hans Hermann retired after setting the fastest lap. Shades of 1908 and 1914 all over and following the sports car successes of 1952.

By 1954 the 220 had been revised to a monocoque body shell on the lines of the 180 but with the six-cylinder engine. The basic saloon had four doors and carried six while the 220S of 1956 was faster and the 220SE that came later in 1958 had fuel injection.

In production form the 300SL carried the factory code W198 and was a coupé model to the firm, the gullwing to the general public. It was not an easy car to drive at high speed due to the swing-axle rear suspension, but it was seldom necessary to reach that limit. The door handle was a neat touch, pressure on the end lifting it out from its recess for use.

The great Juan Manuel Fangio during the 1954 German Grand Prix held on the Nürburgring in which he used the open-body W196. Hermann had a streamliner, and Lang and Kling open cars, but the last lost time due to a stop for fuel and to sort suspension problems and finished fourth while the other two went out. Fortunately Fangio won and went on to the second of his five world titles.

The 180D was listed from 1954 fitted with a 1767cc, four-cylinder, overhead-valve diesel engine in the monocoque body shell in place of the petrol unit. Later, in 1961, a 1988cc overhead-camshaft diesel engine was used to boost the power and performance.

The 300SL was an expensive car to buy and maintain in top condition so the firm introduced the 190SL in this form at the 1954 New York Show with the final form first seen in the following Spring. Built as a Roadster and as a fixed-head coupé by adding a factory hardtop, it lacked the side vents of the 300SL and some of its special style, but filled a need and sold well.

There was never any problem in recognising the 300SL, especially when one of the doors was opened. The spare wheel occupied most of the boot space but this was never a car for going to the shops, while luggage was stowed behind the seats.

Lifting the body of a 300SLR into place in preparation for one of the major sports car races. Under the aluminium was the tubular space frame that carried the eight-cylinder engine developed by stretching that of the W196, and the massive fuel tank for the long-distance events. A single head fairing and cover over the passenger space was used by Fangio and Kling in the Mille Miglia as neither carried a navigator.

The fabled W196 raced by Mercedes-Benz in 1954 and 1955 to take Fangio to two of his world titles. The engine had desmodromic, or positive, valve operation, fuel injection, and was laid far over on one side to reduce height. Inboard front and rear brakes were used at first but some 1955 cars had the fronts outboard.

Right: There was little real difference between the W196 and this 300SLR for the latter used the suspension, brakes, gearbox and engine of the former with the last enlarged from 2497cc to 2982cc. The frame was different to cater for the sports car regulations concerning seats, interior and doors, but remained a tubular space-frame type. Beautifully made, extremely reliable and meticulously prepared, they dominated for two years. A 3.0-litre W196 was also built for one South American race and the team was first, second and fourth, a reminder of Tripoli and 1939.

The 220 ran on to 1955 with its styling a legacy of the prewar 170 in many ways other than it not having separate headlights. Built in saloon, coupé and cabriolet styles, it sold and performed well but was due for a revamp that came in the next year.

The 300 saloon brought a return to prestigious cars for the firm in 1951 and the following year saw the 300C make its debut. It was a rare model with its four-door cabriolet body with barely 700 built in five years, this one from 1955.

The 300SLR in its 1955 form with twin head fairing was effectively the grand prix car with an enlarged engine and sports car body. It kept all the special features that included a mechanism around the gear lever that prevented an incorrect gear change. This was first developed for Stirling Moss and later went on all the racing cars.

The 300SLR as used at Le Mans in 1955 with the air brake raised, a massive fuel filler behind it and Fangio's race number on the side. In the race Fangio battled with Mike Hawthorn's Jaguar but then came the disaster that sent Levegh's Mercedes into the crowd and led to the team's withdrawal.

Left: Having tried an air brake on the roof of a coupé at Le Mans in 1952, the firm came up with this design for 1955 and used it during the race. It was hydraulically operated and lever controlled by the driver, the fuel tank filler cap located under it in some cases.

Fangio's W196 being pushed out for the start of the 1955 British Grand Prix held at Aintree where four Mercedes ran and took the first two places. Fangio finished just behind Stirling Moss who remains unsure as to whether he was gifted the race or was the better man that day as Fangio insisted. Kling and Taruffi were the other two drivers.

Once in production, the 190SL lost the air intake on the bonnet and had the door line altered to a roadster style. This suited the addition of the hardtop that turned it into a coupé, the result proving popular, while the 1.9-litre, four-cylinder, single-cam engine and simpler specification made for a car with line that was much cheaper to buy and easier to maintain than the 300SL.

The stuff of legends, the 300SLR as used by Stirling Moss to win the 1955 Mille Miglia at a record 97.99 mph. The actual car had twin head fairings for much of the success was due to Denis Jenkinson who passengered Moss and relayed signals to him for the full 1,000 miles to indicate corners, speeds, gears and flat-out blind brows.

Left: The 300Sc replaced the 300S late in 1955 and continued in coupé, cabriolet and this roadster forms but built in even more limited numbers. The main engine change was to Bosch fuel injection, while retaining the dry-sump lubrication system, and the series remained rare and expensive with only 200 being built in all.

Stirling Moss and Peter Collins shared this 300SLR in the 1955 Targa Florio which they won despite both drivers having moments of contact with the scenery as the body work confirmed. Fangio and Kling were second so it was a good day for Mercedes.

The 219 was a variant of the 220 that appeared in 1956 as an economy model that kept the 2195cc single-cam six engine but with only one carburettor and less power. A shorter wheelbase, simple trim and only listed in saloon form, it gave low-cost motoring built to the Mercedes standards.

Above: Lowering the body of a 300SL into place onto the tubular space frame at the factory in 1955. The model had its own special build area so lacked the normal production line facilities, the assemblies sitting on rolling support frames. Without computer control to position one part in place above the other, care was needed at this stage to ensure that nothing was damaged.

Right: The W196 in streamlined form that caused such a sensation when it first appeared at the 1954 French Grand Prix to mark the return of Mercedes-Benz to grand prix racing. It was just as radical under the skin and won first time out in France, also at Monza and at an event on the Avus circuit where the fastest lap was by Fangio at 139.1 mph. In 1955 the open cars were used at all events other than Monza.

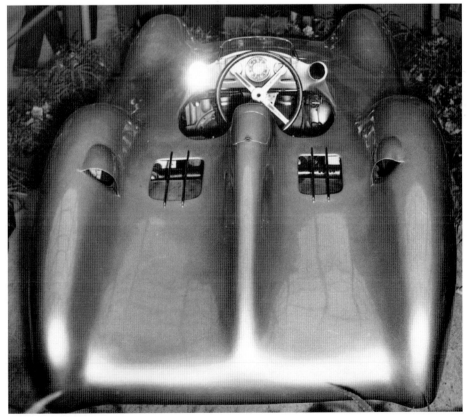

One of the rare 300 Cabriolet D four-door models built from 1952 to 1956 at around 140 per year. These were expensive, luxury cars in their day, well built to high standards with a good performance. The cabriolet style was often the choice of a head of state who could be seen by the people when the sun shone and the top was down.

The 180 cars of 1953 with the monocoque body were known in Germany as 'ponton' which referred to the rounded shape they had and thus, the whole series became the pontoon in Europe and the USA. The 190 succeeded the 180 in 1956 and was joined by this 190D variant two years later, it having a four-cylinder, single-camshaft diesel engine.

Frontal aspect of the 190 that appeared in 1956 with an improved engine and rear suspension to the 180, and distinguished by a new bonnet and grill. It continued in production to 1961, always in saloon form, and as a good, solid, reliable car even if not the most exciting.

In 1957 the 300SL coupé was replaced by this roadster that had more of the line of the 190SL. A factory hardtop was also available to turn the model into a neat coupé and while later models had disc brakes, the early ones used drums all round.

Two Mercedes-Benz owners pictured in a German village during a club rally from Britain to Stuttgart. On the left a 1956 300S coupé and beside it a 1935 500K roadster with both occupants and onlookers enjoying the occasion. The run took four days to complete via Ghent, Spa, Wiesbaden and Wurzburg.

The 190SL for 1958 on show and fitted with the factory hardtop that turned it into a coupé. The car was often referred to as a sheep in wolf's clothing, but it was a reliable sheep, cheap to keep, and the clothes were stylish. There were better cars available at the price, but the 190SL appeal sold over 25,000 units.

The monocoque body of the 190 was much as the 180, but with the grill laid back more, and both models continued on into the 1960s offering basic transport over many years and considerable mileage. Servicing was easy so these models were run until the ancillaries ended their lives, usually leaving the basic mechanics still in action.

In 1957 the 300SL coupé was replaced by the Roadster that remained essentially the same mechanically but had conventional doors with wind-up windows to provide easier access and better ventilation. It was available with a soft top, or this hardtop, and some customers had both, changing them at home to suit the journey and weather at the time. Handling was improved and there were detail changes such as the headlight cover.

There was a new style for 1960 that was quickly adopted by the main range that included this 300SE on view at the 1961 Frankfurt Show. It continued with the 3.0-litre, six-cylinder, single-cam engine but tail fins appeared at the end of the body in a parody of a US trend. Underneath there was fuel injection, self-levelling air suspension and disc brakes.

The older monocoque body form ran on to 1959, this a 220SE coupé able to seat two or four and powered by a 2.2-litre six with fuel injection. Then it was time for a change.

This 220SE cabriolet from 1961 was one of the new line known as 'fin-backs' from the rear body shape. Also built in saloon and coupé forms, all had disc front brakes and were solid, middle-range cars.

A step into the world of the rich, powerful and famous. Heads of state, pop stars and politicians all enjoyed the enormous Mercedes-Benz 600 that came in 1963 powered by a 6.3-litre, V-8, overhead-camshaft engine to waft its 18-foot length along. Every refinement of the period included.

The long, standard 600 brought back memories of the Grosser 770 of the 1930s and it remained in production for some 18 years, during which time 2,677 of them were built. Underneath the impressive skin went a good deal of complication ranging from double disc front brakes to power-assisted seats, windows and doors among other items. The car handled well for such a massive machine and could well exceed 120 mph.

For those to whom the stock 600 was not enough there was also the Pullman with another two feet in length and available with six doors, and this Landaulet that had a folding roof section to show off the important passengers. Owners ranged from Mao Tse-Tung to the Pope plus some who just wanted to show off.

After the 300SL the firm introduced a new form for its sporting cars with this 230SL the first. It kept the familiar camshaft-six engine, with 2.3-litre capacity, but the body had a fresh, elegant line high lighted by the big three-pointed star on the grill. Built as a roadster and this hardtop coupé with a pagoda style for the roof, the car was an improvement on the 190SL in just about every way.

The mid-1960s brought a change to the body style with tail fins removed and the rear smoothed out. The top of the series for those unable to run to a 600 was the 300SE that also came in the longer SEL form and could have a 3.5-litre, V-8 engine fitted. This is the two-door cabriolet, while saloon and coupé bodies were also listed.

The Mercedes-Benz line of models adopted many permutations from 1960 onwards, producing a range of body forms available with various engines. One result was this 1966 250SE that had the 2.5-litre version of the camshaft-six engine fitted with fuel injection and listed with saloon, coupé and cabriolet bodies, although this two-door type was rare.

The fin-back style continued for the late-1960s on this 200D that replaced the 190D and had a 2.0-litre diesel engine offering a modest 60 bhp. While not their most exciting model, it sold well for several years for taxi work and economy motoring.

The 230 was another model that continued to wear fins in the late-1960s, being an enlarged 2.3-litre 220 and only built as a saloon, but well equipped with a good option list and disc front brakes.

The 230S version alone had the vertical headlight clusters and in this case an estate body, a form that was seldom associated with the marque despite the range of commercial vehicles that they produced.

A 250SL of the late-1960s standing on cobbles and among buildings a good deal older than itself. The stylish form of the pagoda roof line was unusual but worked very well in this hardtop coupé. The 2.5-litre version of the six engine pushed it along to 120 mph and there were all-round disc brakes to halt it.

Another permutation in the late-1960s resulted in this 250S that used the existing 146 bhp engine in the four-door saloon body shell. Coupé and cabriolet bodies were also listed and all were available in 250SE form with fuel injection and 170 bhp. All-round disc brakes went on every version.

By the late-1960s the bigger Mercedes saloons were sophisticated luxury cars with improved engines although they still stuck to the single-overhead camshaft, six-cylinder type in the main. A high standard of fixtures and fittings were specified and the result a satisfactory motor car, this one either a 250 or a 280.

Although Mercedes model numbers normally indicated the engine capacity, this was not always so as this 280SE 3.5 coupé demonstrated. While the body and most of the specification remained as it was, the engine was the 3.5-litre, single-camshaft V-8 producing 200 bhp and this boosted the performance to over 125 mph.

Left: At one time the Wankel rotary engine was thought to be the way ahead and many firms spent much time, effort and money endeavouring to develop it to fully practical use. Mercedes-Benz were among them and the C111 was the result, its engine producing plenty of power to drive this gullwing coupé. It remained a concept model with a dozen or so built plus specials for record attempts.

The 300SEL was an impressive car with its 3.0-litre, fuel-injected engine in the long-wheelbase form, but this was much better. Under the bonnet went the 6.3-litre, V-8 from the 600 so 135 mph was on tap. The car is on the Mercedes-Benz test ground banked section whose angle allowed hands-off motoring at 93 mph at the top.

The 280SE 3.5 in its cabriolet form with two doors but able to seat five in its long and graceful body lines. Fast but thirsty to continue the heritage of the prewar 540K but with all the modern safety features and interior fittings.

One of the basic, mid-range Mercedes-Benz saloons of the 1970s that continued to do their work without fuss or bother, day in and day out. This is the 250 with the faithful six-cylinder engine enlarged to 2.8-litre to produce 157 bhp.

Left: The sporting SL series was revised for 1971 and the following year brought this 350SLC on a longer wheelbase to give a true four-seater coupé. The louvre rear window quarters were one result while the 3.5-litre, V-8 engine ensured it had plenty of go.

153

By 1980 this was the form of the 380SLC with its V-8 engine and hardtop coupé body able to accommodate four although cramped in the rear. It offered pleasant, fast transport, especially where only two were going, and had good lines.

One of the estate bodies known as the T-range and thus cars such as the 240TD and 300TD with diesel engines and 230T, 250T and 280TE with petrol, the last also with fuel injection. The range of sizes and comprehensive option list ensured that every need was catered for.

The 450SE set new standards for luxury cars when it appeared in 1973 and it was soon joined by the longer 450SEL. A 4520cc, V-8, overhead-camshaft engine provided the power, a three-speed automatic transmission was used, and the equipment was truly comprehensive.

The sporting coupé came in several capacities and the 350SLC was the smallest in the 1970s but remained a good performer with style and quality in its build and fitments, this a 1975 example.

A new 190 series appeared in 1983 using a 1.9-litre engine to propel the four-door, five-seater saloon and other engines soon followed. By 1986 these included a 2.3-litre unit with twin-overhead camshaft and four valves for each of its four cylinders, the head design by Cosworth and the car the 190E 2.3-16.

By 1987 the lines of this 300SL were beginning to date and what had been fresh was losing its appeal. For all that it, and the smaller 280SL, were fine cars for those seeking a two-door, two-seater convertible, while the style could never be mistaken on the road.

The saloon car of the 1980s was used as the basis of the 380SEC and 500SEC two-door, four-seater coupé models introduced in 1981 and used the same V-8 engines and four-speed automatic transmission. Well built, quality fittings, good handling and a fine line made for a desirable car.

Estate versions of the Mercedes-Benz sold well in the UK and were available for most combinations of model and engine. They had the same options as the saloons and for the 300E this included the firm's automatic four-wheel drive system that put the power where it could be used. This is a mid-range model for the late-1980s.

The model code system was revised for 1994, so this was an E230, and along with other changes the new headlight style was the easiest to spot. The E meant executive class and was available in a variety of style and trim packages.

A 1996 S-class car in Elegance trim. As with the E-class, this S for Saloon series had the same options of style package, the others being Classic, Esprit and Sport. Allied to the option list it allowed the customer to select precisely the car and fittings desired.

The sporting cabriolet series for the 1990s extended from the SL280 with a 24-valve, six-cylinder engine right up to the 48-valve, V-12 SL600 via the SL500 with its V-8 motor. The roll-over bar extended automatically, the top was powered at the press of a button and the cars were true performers in the Mercedes manner.

It was back to the Kompressor for the SLK230, based on the C230K, with an engine-driven supercharger rather than a turbocharger. It went into a two-seater sports coupé body with the usual Mercedes refinements, the result a compact model that was a joy to drive.

INDEX